Behind the Scenes

THEATRE

JUDITH ANDERSON

First published in 2009 by Wayland

Wayland
338 Euston Road
London NW1 3BH

Wayland Australia
Level 17/ 207 Kent Street
Sydney NSW 2000

Editor: Nicola Edwards
Design manager: Paul Cherrill
Designer: Rita Storey

British Library Cataloguing in Publication Data

Anderson, Judith, 1965-
Theatre. - (Behind the scenes)
1. Theatre - Vocational guidance - Juvenile literature
I. Title
792'.0293

ISBN: 978 0 7502 5891 3

The author would like to thank David Buss and Sebastiane Brewer, theatre technicians at the University of Winchester and Kate Raines, Marketing Manager at Theatre Royal Winchester for their helpful comments on the text.

The author and publisher would like to thank the following for permission to reproduce the following photographs in this book:
© Mike Goldwater/Alamy p1 and 21, © Peter Horree/Alamy p2 and 25, © Transtock Inc./Alamy p7, © Jeff Greenberg/Alamy p9, © Gondwanaphoto art/Alamy p18, © David Taylor/Alamy, p26, © Keith Morris/Alamy p27, © Ros Drinkwater/Alamy p28; Matt Cardy/Getty Images p4, Dave M. Benett/Getty Images pp5 and 22, Jeff J Mitchell/Getty Images p6 Jeff J Mitchell/Getty Images p10, Eamonn McCormack/Wirelmage p11, Vince Bucci/Getty Images p12, Jeff J Mitchell/Getty Images p13, Cate Gillon/Getty Images p14, Oli Scarff/Getty Images p16, Stephen Chernin/Getty Images p17, Jim Dyson/Getty Images p29; i-stock p23.
Cover image: Jeff J Mitchell/Getty Images

Printed in China

Wayland is a division of Hachette Children's Books,
an Hachette UK company.
www.hachette.co.uk

Contents

Why theatre?

The lights go down, the audience goes quiet, the curtain goes up... There's nothing quite like the thrill of live theatre. Anything might happen. Will the actors remember their lines? Will the scene changes go smoothly? Will the audience be drawn into the drama unfolding in front of their eyes?

A team effort

As we watch the actors on the stage it is easy to forget that a whole team of people have been working for weeks, months, or even years to bring a production to life. First, writers, directors and producers must decide on a play. Then designers create sets and costumes. Carpenters, scene painters, electricians and prop makers prepare the stage while actors rehearse. Marketing managers advertise the production and box office staff sell tickets.

Then there is the performance itself. Stage managers, wardrobe assistants, lighting technicians and stagehands make sure that props are in place, costumes are laid out and the spotlights are following the actors. Ushers show members of the public to their seats. Bar staff serve drinks in the interval.

A varied cast

A big production in a large theatre employs a wide range of highly specialised professionals for jobs such as make-up, sound production or pyrotechnics (anything to do with fire). In a smaller production or a touring production people are often expected to do more than one job. Actors may help with scene changes

←

This sound technician watches a performance of 'Jack and the Beanstalk' from his sound desk behind the audience.

or costumes, for example. Yet whatever the task, it is essential that everyone views themselves as part of a team whose goal is to stage the best theatrical event possible.

A flexible career

Many people working in theatre are employed on a freelance basis. This means they are paid per production, or sign a temporary contract rather than work as a permanent member of staff. This is particularly the case for creative jobs such as acting, directing, designing – those jobs that change from one production to the next. This way of working requires a flexible, adaptable attitude. There is less job security but possibly more variety and freedom to work on those projects that most interest you.

THINKING AHEAD

• If you like the idea of working in theatre but don't yet know which area you'd like to focus on then get involved in a school or amateur production, apply for work experience with a theatre or volunteer your services as an usher.
• You could also take one of the backstage theatre tours sometimes offered by large theatres. Don't be afraid to ask questions – most people working in theatre are passionate about what they do and are only too happy to pass this on.

'Theatre excludes no-one. Whether you are the audience, the stagehand, the actor, the box office manager, the main actress or the person who sweeps the stage at the end of the show, if there's a part you'd like to play in making theatre, you can trust there'll be a part for you.'

Lucy Neal, co-founder, London International Festival of Theatre.

Theatre management

Every theatre or theatre company needs someone to make decisions. Which plays will be performed? Who will the director be? How will everything be paid for? A chief executive (sometimes known as a managing director) takes overall responsibility for budgets and staff and usually employs a team of people to manage specific areas.

Different types of theatre

Some theatres put on their own productions. They choose the plays, set the budget and hire the directors, designers and other creative and technical staff. A production manager will organise the backstage area and rehearsal space and oversee the construction of sets, costumes, sound and lighting rigs. This type of theatre is called a 'production house'.

Other types of theatre simply provide a venue in which a touring company can stage a play. The theatre invites the touring company to perform and then organises the publicity and sale of tickets. It also provides some technical support, such as with lighting. The touring company will bring its own sets, costumes and stage crew. This kind of theatre is known as a 'receiving house'.

A touring theatre company, on the other hand, is a group of

← *Dancers and musicians from Scottish Ballet rehearse 'The Sleeping Beauty' before going on tour.*

← *'The Phantom of the Opera' has been staged at Her Majesty's Theatre in London since 1986.*

actors, directors and other members, led by a management team, who take their production to a series of different venues. The Royal Shakespeare Company is an example of a theatre company that goes on tour and also has a permanent base at the Royal Shakespeare Theatre in Stratford-upon-Avon.

Finance

Putting on a play or show is an expensive business. Some of this is paid for by selling tickets, programmes, drinks and snacks purchased at the theatre and the sale of items such as posters and t-shirts. However, many theatres and touring companies also depend on grants from the government and sponsorship from businesses that pay to have their name publicised in theatre programmes and on ticket stubs. All of these sources of income are the responsibility of a business development director who plays a crucial role in the success of any theatre production.

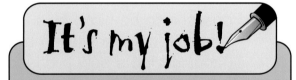

It's my job!

Lucy Neal, co-founder, London International Festival of Theatre.

"Setting up the London International Festival of Theatre was hard work. We travelled around the world, we raised money, we booked the venues and we explained why the shows were extraordinary and why we wanted people to come and see them. We invited shows from Brazil, South Africa, China, Poland, Indonesia, Italy, Vietnam, Palestine, France – from everywhere. In all these countries theatre can look and sound very different, but it's achieving the same thing: telling the story of people's lives."

The director

The director is hired to interpret a specific play and make it relevant and exciting for the audience. He or she is responsible for all the creative aspects of the production. This means working closely with actors and the creative and technical staff behind the scenes.

The director's vision

The director is usually the first person to be hired by a theatre or theatre company when they are considering a new production. A director needs to be someone with the confidence to bring his or her own vision to a play; whether it is a brand-new play or an old play that has been performed thousands of times before. He or she may consult with the writer (the playwright) to get ideas about how the play might be staged. The director will also talk to the designer to discuss the 'look' of the play so that work can begin on sets and costumes. The stage itself is an important consideration – will there be any practical difficulties associated with a particular venue?

THINKING AHEAD

Annie Rigby, Artistic Director of Unfolding Theatre in Newcastle, has this advice: "There is a presumption that if you are a director, you need to know everything about everything, but that's not true. However, you do need to be good at working with people, to fully utilise their knowledge and experience. Don't be afraid to ask for help when you most need it."

Auditions and rehearsals

Next the director must decide on a cast. This usually involves holding auditions to find the right actors for the job. When the actors have been hired the director needs to explain his or her vision for the play and work closely with the actors in rehearsal to coax the very best performances from them. So a director needs to have excellent communication skills as well as creative confidence.

Final adjustments

When the actors have developed their characters and learned their lines, they need to become familiar with the space in which they will perform. As most rehearsal time is spent in a room away from the theatre, this late transition to the stage can be a crucial moment for the director. How will the play 'work' in this new space? Now the costumes, scenery, special effects and lighting are all brought together and the final adjustments are made.

↓ *An actor and a director work together in rehearsal.*

Any questions ?

I want to be a theatre director. What should I do?

- The best preparation for any future director is to watch as many different performances as you can. Ask yourself how you would have staged each production.
- Get involved in live performance as much as possible; act, shift scenery, sit in on rehearsals for your school or college productions or join a youth theatre or an amateur theatre group.
- When you leave school there are many different courses in theatre production on offer – and when you apply for these, all your previous experience will be useful.
- Many directors work as an assistant director first, getting involved in rehearsals and liaising with technical staff before taking creative control of their own productions.
- Be prepared to live and breathe the theatre. You'll need to demonstrate your passion to work in this demanding environment.

An actor's life

What does it take to become an actor? Talent and determination, definitely. But theatre actors also need tremendous physical and mental stamina to be able to perform on stage for two hours or more, night after night, with only one day off a week.

Off the stage

Actors must audition if they want a role in a particular play or show. It is a good idea to do plenty of preparation beforehand – by reading the play if you can, practising scenes and finding out as much as possible about the theatre company that is going to be staging the production.

Once an actor is hired, rehearsals can begin. Rehearsal time for a stage play is usually three to five weeks and involves long days in a rehearsal room with the director and the rest of the cast as well as private preparation, learning lines and developing a character. During this time actors will also attend costume fittings and specialised workshops to prepare for any stage-fighting or dancing.

Any questions

What is an agent and do I need one?

An agent looks after an actor's career, finding out about new plays, talking to casting directors, setting up auditions and, when an actor gets a job, negotiating the pay and expenses. In return, the actor pays the agent a percentage of his or her earnings. It isn't essential for an actor to have an agent but it can be difficult to find out about auditions and negotiate a good rate of pay without one.

← *An actor applies make-up in the dressing room before a dress rehearsal.*

On the stage

Acting requires more than a good memory and an ability to listen to the director. Theatre actors in particular need to be able to connect with their audience, projecting their voice so that hundreds of people can follow what they are saying and creating a compelling presence on stage through their movements and expressions.

Actors also need to be comfortable working as part of a team because they depend on each other for their cues and responses. Most importantly, actors need to be able to summon up the same passion and commitment for every single performance, even if they have played the role hundreds of times already.

An unpredictable career

Theatre actors are almost always freelance, which means they are paid per production, or even per performance. Pay is notoriously low and there are never enough parts for everyone, so there may be long periods when actors are out of work.

Most actors have to earn money doing other jobs outside the theatre, often choosing flexible employment, e.g. as waiting staff, so that they can still attend auditions when they need to. There is little financial security but most theatre actors will say that the thrill of performing to a live audience is what matters most to them.

←

"There are a lot of actors who think you can just go on stage and do it — you can't. You need to project [your voice]. You can give the most amazing performance on stage but if the audience can't hear you, then it's useless," says actor Daniel Radcliffe, shown here performing on stage in London with Joanna Christie.

Theatre design

Every play, every show or piece of street theatre is designed in some way. This means that someone has thought about how it will look and how it will work. Costumes, sets and scenery, props, lighting and special effects must all be considered as they help to create setting and atmosphere – the world of the play.

The designer

The designer meets with the director at the start of a new production to discuss the 'look' for the set – the concept, the colours and the lighting as well as the background scenery.

Then the designer makes sketches, draws plans and builds scale models of the set to see how the stage can be used most effectively and to work out how the scene changes might take place.

THINKING AHEAD

Many designers have a relevant BTEC HND or a degree in theatre design, 3-D design or theatre production. However, practical experience is just as important and people who can demonstrate their design input in amateur theatre are more likely to gain work experience in a professional theatre or find a job as a designer's assistant or a prop maker.

← *A model of the set for the 75th Annual Academy Awards (the 'Oscars') is unveiled during a press conference in Hollywood, California.*

↑ *The designer Anthony Lamble used an old camper van for the Globe Touring Company's production of 'Romeo and Juliet'. It served as the backdrop, the entrance and exit points for the actors, the balcony, the lighting rig and even the dressing room!*

A creative approach

Theatre designers need to have a strong creative sense, and the vision to pull many separate elements together to make a distinctive statement about the play. However, often they are working to a very tight budget, or they have to create a set that can be taken apart, transported to many different theatres and reconstructed quickly as part of a touring production. Sometimes props and costumes have to be multifunctional, and this requires great ingenuity. The designer passes his or her designs to the production team which includes costume makers, scene painters and set builders.

It's my job!

Corina Bona, freelance costume and set designer

"First I sit down with a director to break down the script and discuss ideas. I then do research, such as the period a play is set, and get together images that inspire me from reading the script. Then I sit down with the production team to discuss budgets and what sort of design we could achieve. Next I put together a scale model of the stage set and costume drawings. I then put everything together for the set and make sure the actors are comfortable in their costumes. I'm involved until the opening night and then I leave."

Wardrobe, props and make-up

Tailors, wig and hat makers, make-up artists, prop makers and prop buyers all help to turn the designer's ideas into reality. Whether the play is set in medieval York, 19th century Paris or contemporary India, the actors must look right and wear clothes and make-up that will withstand the rigours of live performance.

↑ *A wig artist fits a wig on an actor at the Courtyard Theatre in Stratford-Upon-Avon, England.*

Research

Anyone working in props and wardrobe will be expected to carry out detailed research into the period in which the play is set and its culture to make sure that everything the audience sees is as authentic as possible. So a costume maker working on clothes for a play set in the 1940s, for example, might look at old photographs and paintings, read diaries and magazines from the period, talk to those who remember what it was like and visit museums to view items of clothing on display. The prop buyer's job is to find and purchase items such as old telephones or crockery that help to recreate the era on the stage.

It's my job!

Nicky Holderness, Head of Props, Royal National Theatre, London

"The most challenging aspect of working in props is the huge variety of skills which are needed. Once you have mastered upholstery, furniture making, mould making, sculpture, painting, sewing, dying, metal work and puppet making you then often have to combine them all into a prop which also has to be danced on, collapse and then burst into flames."

Workshops and maintenance

A large producing theatre will have its own workshops where costumes and props are made, fitted and maintained. Maintenance is a constant concern during a production as buttons fall off, clothes get dirty and props are smashed or damaged. At the end of the run the costumes and props will be cleaned, catalogued and stored.

Skills and training

Tailors, wig and hat makers, make-up artists and prop makers generally follow a training course or specialised degree before applying for jobs in the theatre. The work is highly skilled and training may continue on the job once a graduate is taken on as an assistant to a more experienced person. However, it helps if you have a keen eye for detail and the ability to use materials creatively.

Any questions

I want to be a make-up artist in the theatre. What sort of training do I need?

A good first step would be to take a general beauty or hair course and get some work experience in a beauty salon. However, more specialised courses such as a BTEC in production arts or media make-up are seen as increasingly important by employers in the industry. And of course, any work experience you can get with an established theatre make-up artist will be invaluable. Hairdressing and wig-fitting experience will also increase your 'employability' and give you skills you can fall back on in between theatre jobs.

Theatre technicians

Theatre technicians ensure the smooth running of all the technical aspects of a theatre production. They operate the spotlights, suspend and secure the scenery, control the sound effects and make sure that all the equipment is safe and working properly. The technicians are responsible for the maintenance of equipment and its operation during rehearsals and performances. They usually report to a production manager or technical manager.

The touring production

When a theatre production goes on tour it has a small technical crew to accompany it from venue to venue to ensure that sound and lighting requirements are met and that sets

and sound and lighting rigs are taken down and rebuilt correctly each time. The touring technicians must work with the technicians employed by the venue to coordinate the all-important 'fit-up' of scenery and equipment on arrival, and the 'get out' when it is time to leave. Both sets of technicians must work together to ensure the smooth running of the performance itself.

Lighting and sound

The number of technicians involved in any production will depend on its size and the size of the venue. The chief electrician is usually known as the chief LX and he or she will be responsible for all the electrical equipment as well as programming and operating the lighting desk and controlling the sound during the

←

A lighting technician at work during a rehearsal of a production of 'The Snowman' at the Peacock Theatre in London.

show. A large production will employ many technicians to set up equipment, create special sound effects, control stage mechanics such as revolving stages, and so on.

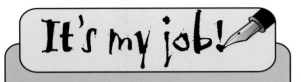

It's my job!

Rachel Fox, Chief LX at Theatre Royal Winchester, UK

"At the moment I am busy rigging, focusing and plotting the lighting for the winter season's pantomime. Lighting can enhance or detract from a show, so it's critical to get it right."

Getting involved

Receiving theatres often need volunteers to help with 'fit-ups' and 'get outs' – it can be a great way to get a foot in the door, meet technicians and see what goes on behind the scenes. Many technicians gain their first experience of lighting as a 'follow spot' – the person who operates the spotlight that follows an actor around on the stage. You'll need to be aged at least 16 to volunteer, but you don't need any qualifications and it provides the perfect opportunity to watch, ask questions and learn as much as you can!

THINKING AHEAD

- All sorts of technical training is available for particular skills such as wiring or sound engineering, but many theatre technicians start out by learning on the job before developing a specialism.
- You will need to be flexible, adaptable and practical – when a bulb blows mid-show or the bolt for a rig is missing, you'll need to know immediately what to do.
- A driving licence is often useful, and a short course in First Aid and other health and safety qualifications such as Portable Appliance Testing (PAT) may give you a step up to that first job.

← A technician checks the lighting for the New York production of 'Hairspray'.

Production specialists

While every production needs people to control light and sound, many require a wider range of technical expertise. The sets themselves need carpenters, welders and artists to build and paint them. Then there are the firearms and combat specialists, pyrotechnic experts and puppeteers who deliver their own particular brand of theatrical effect.

⬆ A scene painter works backstage before the scenery is placed in position.

Set builders and scenic painters

Sets and scenery are usually constructed by carpenters and metal workers using a 1:25 scale three-dimensional model provided by the designer. Most theatres don't have the space for workshop areas on site. Carpenters and metal workers are more likely to work on the sets elsewhere and they are not fully constructed until they are brought in and fitted up on the stage, ready for the performance. However, a large producing theatre will have extensive workshops with permanent staff and sets constantly under construction.

It's my job!

Hilary Vernon-Smith, Head Scenic Artist at the Royal National Theatre in London
"When the set has been built by the carpenters and metal workers we then texture and paint it – if it is to be a naturalistic piece we probably age it. If it is a painted cloth backdrop we square up the reference and then transfer the drawing square by square. At the National Theatre we also carve and sculpt, which is slightly unusual for scenic artists."

Stage crew

Stage crew, sometimes known as stagehands, rig or suspend the scenery before a show, store it and repair it between performances, ensure that scene changes take place smoothly during a show and operate any mechanical components such as trap doors, moving stages and other hydraulic equipment. More experienced crew may also operate the systems that control suspended or 'flown' scenery as it is lowered down to the stage or lifted up into the 'fly tower' – a storage area above the stage.

Stunts and safety

Sometimes specialists are hired to create a very specific effect on the stage such as an explosion or a flying sequence or a fight scene. They may be used to working in film and TV too, as theatre alone may not provide sufficient work. If you are interested in any kind of stunt work or stage effects you'll need to be fit, agile, adaptable and you'll also need to demonstrate that you are very safety conscious – you cannot take risks that might endanger the actors, the crew or the audience.

THINKING AHEAD

"As part of their theatre studies our students learn that all stage combat has to be approved by a trained and qualified stunt specialist – actors need to understand how to deliver a stage punch during an adrenalin-fuelled live performance without risking the safety of all concerned."

David Buss, Senior Theatre Technician, University of Winchester.

← *Stagehands rehearse scene changes to make sure everything works smoothly.*

The stage manager

Lights and sound, scene changes and curtains, actors and props – will everything be in the right place, at the right time? The stage manager is the person who organises all these different elements in the run-up to a performance. The deputy stage manager is the person who coordinates the performance itself.

A managing role

The stage manager's job is largely office-based. He or she will prepare staff schedules for the production team and organise the arrival ('fit up') and departure ('get out') of any touring production. Stage managers book rehearsal rooms, ensure that sets and props are brought in as and when they are needed and deal with any problems to do with the theatre building.

The deputy stage manager

The deputy stage manager (DSM) plays a vital role in any production. During the rehearsal period the DSM is responsible for the rehearsal room, setting up the space with any props required, providing the actors with scripts and making sure they are there on time. He or she will then sit in on all rehearsals, marking up the script according to the director's instructions with careful notes for scene changes, actors'

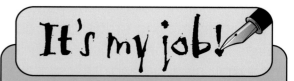

It's my job!

Claire Essex, a freelance ASM

"Before the show I come in and reset from the previous show. This involves resetting props and costumes to their starting positions and making the food and drink used on stage. Once we have set up we always do a 'shout check' to ensure that everything is in its correct place and nothing has been moved since we set it. My day ends when I've mopped up the fake blood after the show. My basic hours are 46 hours per week over six days, plus overtime. It's not easy having a life outside work!"

movements, lighting cues and so on. This is known as 'blocking' the script.

The DSM must also ensure the smooth running of every single live performance. This involves following a marked script known as a 'prompt' script, using headphones

This deputy stage manager is liaising with technicians during a show.

and a microphone to communicate with different technicians around the theatre. He or she will cue lights, sound and special effects, prompt actors when they forget their lines and deal with any emergencies behind the scenes.

The job is demanding and exhausting as the DSM is often the last person to go home after a show. However, he or she is at the heart of any production, acting as the link between its creative and technical elements.

Assistant stage managers

A large production will employ a number of assistant stage managers (ASMs) who are responsible for preparing the stage, ensuring that all props and consumable items such as food or drink are in place,

and resetting the stage at the end of each performance.

Any questions ?

Is being in stage management a stable career?

Most ASMs and DSMs are hired per production and work freelance, touring with a big show from venue to venue. However, the stage manager is more likely to be permanently employed by a theatre as his or her knowledge of the theatre building is vital for coordinating all the different technical elements. Stage management is a clearly defined career in theatre and most new ASMs will have taken a diploma or degree in Stage Management. However it is just as important to gain as much practical experience as possible in student and amateur productions.

Marketing

Marketing is crucial to every theatre and theatre production. Without ticket sales, the production makes no money. Without an audience, the theatre has no reason to exist. So while the director and actors rehearse and the technical team prepares, the marketing department promotes the theatre's activities and develops strategies to bring in the paying public.

Press and publicity

Most theatres have a press and publicity team within their marketing department whose job it is to inform the media and the public about upcoming productions and events. A press officer will write press releases for newspapers, TV and radio, contact journalists about editorial coverage and arrange publicity stunts such as photocalls and interviews with the principal actors.

THINKING AHEAD

Most marketing, publicity and box office/ticket sales jobs offer a regular salary and relatively regular hours. If you don't want the uncertainty of a freelance career but love the idea of working in a busy theatre, have strong writing and speaking skills, aren't afraid of using IT and enjoy being part of a team then a job in the marketing department might be for you. If you're not sure then try volunteering first – many marketing departments welcome volunteers to help with post and administration.

Robbie Williams and Jonathan Wilkes pose with their guests for the press at the Palace Theatre in Manchester, England, during the press night for the production of 'We Will Rock You'.

Print and send

The marketing manager's job is to organise the design and printing of brochures, posters and other promotional material. He or she will have to draw up mailing lists of potential audience members and ensure that information is sent to them.

Attracting sponsors

Ticket sales are rarely sufficient to cover all the expenses of putting on a production and maintaining the theatre building. A further aspect of the marketing department's role is that of increasing the profile of the theatre and attracting sponsors who pay to be associated with it. Sometimes the marketing department will run a campaign to raise funds for specific repairs or refurbishment through donations from well-wishers and local businesses.

← *A theatre's marketing manager liaises closely with the box office manager to keep an eye on ticket sales, track audience numbers and organise any special offers such as reduced rates for school groups.*

It's my job!

Kate Raines, Communications and Strategic Marketing Manager, Theatre Royal Winchester, UK

"Our programme encompasses many artistic strands including drama, physical theatre, dance, music and children's theatre with up to 200 shows a year. My job includes overseeing the box office, maintaining databases for direct mail, producing the season brochure, liaising with the chief executive about sponsorship and development, organising press and advertising campaigns, maintaining the website and, of course, working within a budget. It's an exciting time as the nature of marketing is shifting to digital media such as web, email, SMS and social networking sites, in addition to more traditional marketing tools. The job is constantly evolving and no two days are ever alike!"

Box office and front of house

Theatre staff who have most contact with members of the public are either selling tickets to them, dealing with enquiries or assisting them during their visit to the theatre.

Box office

The box office is the ticket office of a theatre, selling tickets and dealing with enquiries from members of the public. While many theatres also use external ticket agencies to handle the volume of enquiries, they generally maintain a small ticket office within the theatre itself. The box office is still the public face of the theatre and employees need to be polite and knowledgeable about the theatre's programme of events.

Front of house

Theatre staff who come into contact with the audience before, during and after a performance are known as front of house staff. Front of house includes ushers, bar staff, ticket collectors, shop staff, cloakroom attendants and information assistants. The front of house manager recruits and supervises front of house staff, including any volunteers, and deals with complaints from members of the public as well as liaising with food and drink suppliers, cleaners and so on.

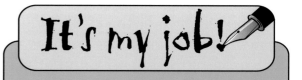

Virginie Clarke studied theatre at university and now works as a tour guide at the Royal National Theatre, giving backstage tours to members of the public. She says: "I was particularly interested in the idea of taking people backstage and helping them discover people and parts of the theatre they hadn't even imagined were there. What's great about the theatre is that it changes constantly, which keeps my job interesting. Its challenges are usually related to customers who might be upset about being late, or booking the wrong tickets. We sometimes have to deal with people in the worst of moods and try to help them while staying calm ourselves."

The box office at the Shaftsbury Theatre in London.

Employment prospects

The box office and front of house areas are both likely to have a full-time manager. Ticket sales assistants and bar staff may also be permanently employed by the theatre, but many venues supplement their permanent staff by hiring temporary staff at busy times. They also use volunteers to act as ushers and ticket collectors who usually get to watch the performances for free.

Some use box office and front of house work as a stepping stone to other types of theatre job, while others make a career out of working in these areas – dealing with people, seeing the shows and getting the theatre buzz while having the benefit of permanent employment.

THINKING AHEAD

Volunteering or getting a part-time job in a box office or as an usher is a great way to build up work experience within the theatre and find out more about the different jobs available. The late summer is a good time to apply because the Christmas holiday period tends to be the busiest time for many theatres. You'll need to be presentable, friendly, calm and helpful. Don't forget to show your interest in the theatre and its productions!

Theatre in education

Has a theatre company ever visited your school to put on a show or run a workshop? Maybe you've visited a theatre on a school trip or taken a drama course? All of these activities make a link between theatre and education and provide opportunities for a variety of careers.

Visiting schools

Some theatre companies visit schools to run drama workshops in which pupils can take part, learning about a particular play, or a period in time, or using drama to explore topical issues such as bullying or relationships. These touring companies may form an outreach arm of a larger company, or they may exist solely to bring theatre into schools.

Community work

Other theatre companies may work with specific groups such as young adults, adults with learning difficulties or people confined to hospitals or care homes. These community theatre companies provide opportunities for learning, social interaction, therapy and personal development through the pleasure and discipline of taking part in a performance.

↑ *A youth theatre group in rehearsal.*

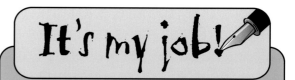

It's my job!

Speakeasy Theatre Company, based in Leicester, uses drama workshops and performance to answer specific educational needs in primary and secondary schools. Bob Christer of Speakeasy says: "One day I could be pretending to be a Tudor director, and the next I could be delivering a substance abuse workshop to secondary school children."

Getting involved

Theatre in education companies are generally very small, with a director or manager and a handful of actors who organise their own props, costumes, make-up and any technical equipment they require.

Members of the company may have traditional acting backgrounds, or they may have trained as teachers, community workers or counsellors or have expertise in areas such as history or environmental issues. All, however, need to be confident communicators who can respond quickly to the needs of their particular audience. The budget for any theatre in education work is always limited and pay is relatively low but the rewards come from seeing the audience interact and learn.

Any questions ?

Why do theatres have education officers?

Many theatres depend on financial grants from government agencies such as the Arts Council as well as the income they receive from ticket sales and sponsors. In order to receive these grants, theatres are expected to offer educational opportunities to the local community in the form of school outreach programmes, drama classes, holiday workshops and so on. The education officer's job is to ensure that such educational opportunities are available, that they are properly staffed and advertised and that they complement the theatre's other activities.

← *This actor is working with children at a school in Wales.*

Street theatre

Street theatre is any dramatic performance that takes place outside, on the street, without the need for a theatre building. Fast, colourful, unpredictable – it often depends on audience participation (and the weather) for its success.

Street festivals

Most street theatre takes place within an organised festival such as the Edinburgh Fringe Festival, when many different acts perform throughout Scotland's capital city in August each year. Performers are usually invited by the festival's artistic director. Sometimes a street theatre company may be given a commission – that is, asked to create a new performance specifically for the event. Where work is commissioned, the artists are likely to be paid a fee. However, many street theatre performers depend on voluntary contributions from the audience on the day.

Small scale...

Some street theatre involves a single actor, clown or mime artist. The performers' costs are low but their income may depend on the goodwill of their audience. They may have to travel extensively between locations. The bonus for any performer is the opportunity to work independently, improvise, hone their skills and get instant feedback from a responsive crowd.

← *A street performer interacts with passers-by in Grafton Street, Dublin.*

...or giant-sized!

Other street theatre can be fabulously large-scale – the picture below shows a street theatre spectacular called 'The Sultan's Elephant' which took place in central London in 2006. A French street theatre company called *Royal de Luxe* created enormous mechanically-operated puppets that walked through the city, delivering a drama that unfolded over a four-day period. This piece of theatre took four years to prepare and involved designers, mechanists, carpenters, painters, costume makers, actors, lawyers, accountants, publicists, producers and security staff. It was paid for out of government money and brought to the UK by a production company called Artichoke.

THINKING AHEAD

Street theatre companies and solo performers generally require a licence to perform to the public outdoors. If you want to perform in the street, either as a busker (with a hat or a box for contributions from the public) or as part of an organised theatre group you will need to check with the local council and apply to them for permission. If you don't have a licence you may be stopped from performing by the police.

↓ *An episode from 'The Sultan's Elephant', performed over four days on the streets of London in 2006.*

Glossary

agent someone who sets up auditions and negotiates salaries for actors in exchange for a percentage of their earnings

auditions when actors, dancers and musicians perform (audition) in front of a director or producer in order to get hired

backstage the part of a theatre the audience cannot see from their seats; the area behind the stage

'blocking' adding the director's instructions to the script during rehearsals

box office the place where theatre tickets are sold

cast the actors, singers and dancers in a play or show

crew the people working backstage during a performance; technicians and stagehands

cues theatre timings; the moment when an actor speaks or a spotlight changes colour or music starts or a special effect takes place

designers people who create the 'look' for a play or a show; they design the costumes, the set, the props or the scenery

director the director is in charge of all the creative aspects of a production, briefing designers, guiding the actors in rehearsals and making sure they understand his or her vision for the play

dressing room the place where performers dress and prepare for a show

'fit-up' when all the scenery and equipment for a particular show is brought into the theatre building and set up for the first performance

freelance not permanently employed by a company; someone who works on short-term contracts for a variety of employers

front of house theatre staff who help members of the audience before and after a performance; ushers, cloakroom attendants, bar staff, programme sales staff

'get out' when all the scenery and equipment for a particular show is dismantled and taken out of the theatre building

grants money given by government or a charity to help a theatre or a theatre company; often for a specific purpose such as building repairs

interval a pause in a performance to allow for scene changes and for audiences to take a break

marketing anything to do with promoting a show and making money for the theatre; publicity, selling tickets and finding new ways to raise funds

playwright the person who writes the play; the author of the play

press release information sent out to newspapers, TV and radio; a way to publicise a new show

producing theatres theatres that put on their own plays and shows

props any item that can be moved on stage during a performance; furniture, food, books, weapons and so on

pyrotechnics anything to do with fire such as explosions or fireworks

receiving house a theatre that invites touring companies to bring their plays and shows to its stages

rigs scaffolding and wiring for lighting, sound and scenery

sponsorship funds in exchange for publicity. A business might help pay for a particular event and and in return get the company's name printed in programmes or on tickets

stage the area in which a theatre performance takes place

stagehands people who assist technicians and deputy stage managers by shifting scenery and props

stage management organising everything necessary for the smooth running of a show, from scripts and rehearsal rooms to scene changes, props, and the actors' and technicians' cues

street theatre live, open air performance in a public place; usually free, though audiences may be asked to make a donation

touring company a group that travels from theatre to theatre, performing in different venues

Further information

The Creative and Media Diploma

The Diploma is a qualification for 14 to 19 year-olds which combines classroom-based study with practical hands-on work experience. It enables you to find out more about the careers you're interested in without having to commit to one of them. Find out more information about the Creative and Media Diploma at:
http://yp.direct.gov.uk/diplomas/subjects/Creative_Media/index.cfm

Theatre qualifications and training

Most people beginning a career in theatre have a university degree or technical qualification that demonstrates their commitment and shows that they have grasped the basic skills. Universities, colleges and drama schools offer a wide variety of courses in stage management, theatre production, lighting and sound, scenic/prop construction and theatre design.

It is possible to find work as a stage hand or 'follow spot' without any qualifications, but taking a course of some sort will help you progress into more specialised technical theatre work.

Books

Working in Show Business: Behind-the-scenes Careers in Theater, Film and Television by Lynne Rogers (Backstage Books, 1998)

Careers in the Theatre by Jean Richardson (Kogan Page Ltd, 1998)

Websites

www.getintotheatre.org
This site is managed by the Arts Council and is part of a theatre initiative aimed specifically at young adults aged between 14 and 25. It is full of tips, information and career guides as well as interactive options such as emailing questions, playing games and getting advice about your CV. Don't miss it!

www.nationaltheatre.org.uk/discover
Go to 'Online Tour' for a guided tour of all departments at the National Theatre and interviews with the different people who work there.

www.thestage.co.uk/connect/
This website for the entertainment industry is full of information and facts about jobs in the theatre; click on 'How To Guides' or 'Frequently Asked Questions' or 'Focus' for frequently updated advice and insight into specific careers.

Index

Numbers in **bold** refer to pictures.

Behind the Scenes

Contents of titles in the series:

WAYLAND